W9-DDS-900

The Soldier's Manual

The Soldier's Manual

Michael Bedell

Copyright © 2019 by Michael Bedell.

ISBN:	Hardcover	978-1-7960-2224-7
	Softcover	978-1-7960-2223-0
	eBook	978-1-7960-2222-3

All rights reserved. No part of this book may be reproduced or transmitted in any form or by any means, electronic or mechanical, including photocopying, recording, or by any information storage and retrieval system, without permission in writing from the copyright owner.

The views expressed in this work are solely those of the author and do not necessarily reflect the views of the publisher, and the publisher hereby disclaims any responsibility for them.

Any people depicted in stock imagery provided by Getty Images are models, and such images are being used for illustrative purposes only.
Certain stock imagery © Getty Images.

Print information available on the last page.

Rev. date: 04/16/2019

To order additional copies of this book, contact:
Xlibris
1-888-795-4274
www.Xlibris.com
Orders@Xlibris.com
793071

CONTENTS

Preface vii

Acknowledgments ix

Chapter I

The Blessed Life 1

The Enemy at the Gate 4

Authority over All 6

Chapter II

The New Birth...13

Out of Control 17

Red Alert...20

Sinful Passions 23

Chapter III

The Messenger 29

The Family Business 33

Pharaoh of the Fleshhook..37

Crossing the Barriers into the Dimension of Truth...........................42

Chapter 7 51

Esau's Values 55

The Devastation of Accusation..62

Index..69

Preface

This book is dedicated to all the disciples and warriors who have withstood persecutions and tribulations in and out of the prison of their minds. They were plotted against, betrayed by friends, even sold into bondage for a few pieces of silver and gold. Why? All because they would not and could not keep quiet about what God had done for them and what He could do for you. These same people today put in long hours on the battlefield, tirelessly and effortlessly fighting in daily struggles to keep the truth from being distorted and to keep evidence from being suppressed and tampered with. Remember that war is always being waged by the one who stands in the darkness of the shadows, sending his troops forth to attack in places where you would least expect to have your armor on—places like the neighborhood grocery store, the Laundromat, the workplace, the schools, the hospitals, and even the church by way of false prophets. These places are strategically chosen. Win-lose ratios are examined. Subjects are studied. Time slots are picked. If you think we are kidding, just look around you and ask yourself, Why did someone go postal today, or why did some kid feel like it would be a good thing to take a pistol to school and shoot someone, fixing his lunch bag, consisting of two bologna and cheese sandwiches, an apple, an orange, a can of soda, a TEC-9, and an extra clip? And don't forget a piece of coconut cake, a grenade, and some napkins. This is the acknowledgment of how real the threat is on the battlefield. This is your warning to be aware that there is an enemy of the state. Be ye forewarned that there is an enemy at your gate. And in order to stay alert for the sake of yourself and your loved ones, to be able to sustain injury and rebound as soon as you get knocked down, you need a soldier's manual. In the book of St. Matthew, Jesus said to His disciples, "Behold I send you out as sheep in the midst of wolves. Therefore be wise as serpents and harmless as doves" (10:16). And in the Second Epistle of Paul the Apostle to Timothy, the apostle said, "You therefore must endure hardship as a good soldier of Jesus Christ" (2:3).

Read the Acts of the Apostles and their missionary journeys. The eyewitness accounts are of epic proportion as these men were in and out of grave, life-threatening situations and unimaginable perils in their attempts to preach the gospel of Christ crucified and the Holy Ghost boldly and with no shame with the help of their fellow soldiers, not knowing what they would encounter from town to town. But through the grace of God and their faith, they received power to be able to teach, preach, and heal all kinds of sickness and all kinds of diseases among the people. People who were afflicted with torments and those who were possessed by demons, epileptics, and paralytics were healed. These men of God withstood strong opposition from those neighborhood deceivers and others preaching smooth words to the people (Isa 30:10, Rom 16:18). The apostles became town enemies. The deceivers and smooth talkers' platforms were destroyed by the Word of God, and they could no longer work. They couldn't pay the town's soldiers (police) their shakedown fee. The town's soldiers couldn't pay the emperor's men (chief of police), and the chief of police couldn't pay the emperor. Kind of sounds like today, doesn't it? Wherever the saints went, they turned wicked environment upside down (Acts 17:6).

When you get up in the morning, open your soldier's manual and let it serve as your guide throughout the day to instructions and directions on how to walk, how to talk, and how to cope with everyday situations. It is no secret what God can do. What He's done for others, He'll do for you. Be armed and dangerous; know your soldier's manual. Don't leave home without it. And never lend it out to anyone for any reason.

Bedell Group Initiative

Acknowledgments

I'd like to thank these very special people in my life for being constant sources of encouragement, love, and motivation.

A very special thanks to my wife, Regina E. Bedell; my pastor, Reverend Snirly Fred Simpson; Apostle L. A. Anderson; Archbishop Rodger Philips; Dean Henry; and the Chicago Baptist Institute (2015).

Bedell Group Initiative

Chapter I

The Blessed Life
The Enemy at the Gate
Authority over All

The Blessed Life

In these past few years, I've had the opportunity to dialogue with people from just about every walk of life. And one thing I've learned about my brothers and sisters is that we are all quick to adopt catchphrases that we hear without any form of investigation as to their meanings or their spirits. The older brother of Jesus and leader of the Jerusalem Council, the apostle James, wrote in his epistle a very noteworthy saying in the first chapter, in the twenty-second through the twenty-fifth verse. In verse 22, the apostle says, "Be doers of the word and not hearers only deceiving yourselves." Verse 23: "For if anyone is a hearer of the word and not a doer, he is like a man observing his natural face in a mirror." Verse 24: "For he observes himself, goes away and immediately forgets what kind of man he was." Verse 25: "But he who looks into the perfect law of liberty and continues in it, and is not a forgetful hearer but a doer of the work. This one will be blessed in what he does."

Here's a good example: a very common phrase you hear nowadays when you ask someone how they're doing is for them to respond and say, "I'm blessed." Two words—one thought gravely misrepresented. In other words, implied but not applied. Do you know anyone like that? Chances are, you used to be the same way. *I'm blessed, but I don't have a car like my neighbor. But I got a car. I'm blessed, but I don't have a house like my neighbor. But I got a roof. I'm blessed, but I don't have a closet full of Sean John, Russell Simmons, or Yves Saint Laurent. But nevertheless, I got clothes on my back and shoes on my feet. I'm blessed, but I don't shop at PayMore. But I'm blessed because I can shop at Payless.* You're living in a blessed atmosphere, but you're shutting off the oxygen supply to the heart by the delusion of denial and bad company corrupting good habits (1 Cor 15:33). Don't say it if you don't mean it. You don't realize how blessed you aren't by association with contamination. Let us go on to be creatures of habit. And the best habit to have is knowledge. You might say, How can knowledge be a habit? It is when it becomes a practice. Let your habit develop into a have-it. So when you walk, walk like you have it. When you talk, talk like you have it. When you stand, stand like you have it. And when you sit, sit like you have it. Practice the habit of having the living life blessed, then you'll know you're living life blessed. The psalmist wrote in the first Psalms that this is not by chance or occurrence; this happens all day every day. "Blessed *is* the man" with the emphasis on *is*. This life is a posture, and this posture is a perspective. And this represents our state of being, which defines our active roles in life, who we are, and whose we are. How are you walking in this life? I would hope not in the counsel of the ungodly. How is your standing among your peers? One would hope it's not in the pathway of sinners. How is your seating arrangement in life? Is it the mourner's bench or a barstool?

Have you ever seen a saint with a physical condition that has over time affected their stance? Draw near and listen to their testimony, and you're sure to hear them say that no matter how it looks, God told the apostle Paul, "My grace is sufficient for you no matter what you might appear to be going through." Their light is bright because they're living the life that God gave them, and they're thankful to be afflicted with blessings every day.

I was watching a television program one evening about a third-world country, and I saw people with children. And I heard them say sometimes, "We don't have enough food to eat or enough water to drink." I said to myself, "Listen to these people. Don't they know they are blessed, even if it's just to have one another?" When I wake up in the morning, I'm blessed. I have the function of my limbs. I'm blessed.

I'm not launching an attack on these organizations. I'm just saying that sometimes, people need to be told that they're blessed although they have less. Sometimes people need to be shown they're blessed by the testimonies of the scriptures. Jesus said in the Gospels, "If you truly love me, feed my lambs and take care of my sheep so that they'll know their lives are blessed in a society that could care less."

The Enemy at the Gate

Satan is sweeping through your city or town, seeking to devour those who simply refuse to thank God for waking up this morning and face whatever the day may bring. Factor this: with the situation you are in right now, no matter how it may appear, you have to wake up to it and face it. But do you know that in the hours you slept, your new blessing was already waiting for you? But the houseman of hell wants you to think otherwise. He doesn't want you to thank your Father Jehovah for providing you with one more chance and thank Him for the breath of His mercy. Did you know the devil starts his day out on that same source of oxygen as you and me? But we are continually urged by the radio, the television, and the media to be in the now and begin our day another way instead of with the way and by the way. In a world of priorities, is giving thanks and thanksgiving our number 1 priority these days? If not, check your surroundings, beginning with your house and church, and you'll see that you could have a visitor—a sort of unwelcome guest. Check underneath your bed, your closets, the bathroom, the kitchen, and most of all, your heart; and you'll see that you have an unwelcome guest. In the book of Noah, his wife and sons and their wives entered the ark the day of the flood that cleansed the earth. Unbeknownst to the family of eight, there was a spirit that crept in unawares. After it rained on the earth for 150 days and things were back to normal, the demonic spirit corrupted the weak link (HAM), which resulted in a family curse. (For more, read the story of Noah and the eight.)

Put this on your radar. The enemy at the gate is sweeping through your city with big guns loaded with such ammo as lust of the flesh, lust of the eyes, and pride of this life. We must know that God doesn't permit Satan to do no more than you permit Satan to do to you. God is the provider, not the denier. He gives the blessing that Satan tries to lessen.

In the Second Epistle to the Corinthians 4:18, we are told "not to look at the things that are seen but at the things that are unseen for the things which are seen are temporary but the things which are not seen are eternal." You might not be able to see your enemy but know he's there, disguised and hiding in waiting to attack you on all fronts. Saints let me remind and encourage while today is today (Heb 3:13) to watch, fight, and pray that the enemy isn't sleeping with you, sleeping with your husband, sleeping with your wife, or sleeping with your son or daughter. Watch. And to you, all I say again watch.

Authority over All

No other book in the Gospels provides a more compelling narrative about the authority of King Jesus than the book of Matthew and his stunningly captivating Sermon on the Mount—a sermon that would be remembered and talked about for ages.

Here, Matthew establishes the fact that Jesus assuredly was the one the Old Testament prophets said would come. They said He would come and lead His people to victory over sin and temptation and the world. Jesus would go on to preach and explain how to have access to (Rom 5:2) and live as citizens of the heavenly kingdom of God. Let's talk about the Son of man and the authority bestowed on Him by His father and how it applies to your life and mine.

First, let's look at the authority. The Greek way to say *authority* is *exousia* (ex-oo-see-ah), and if we examine its many definitions, there's one that sums up all the rest by saying, "The power of one whose will and commands must be obeyed by others" (references the strong, exhaustive concordance of the Bible, page 92 in the Greek version).

Jesus is that person with authority. Therefore, I am a person with authority because I am under authority. And when I play the man, I put on Jesus (Rom 13:14) and wear the cloths of the authority given to me by the authority Himself.

Jesus said in the Gospel of John 14:12, "Anyone who has faith in me will do what I have been doing and greater things." In the Gospel of Luke, Jesus said, "Do occupy till I come or in other words, do business until I return." That means He left you and me empowered with authority to stamp out sickness in our lives, authority to cast out demons in our lives, authority to reign over sin in our lives. And with authority comes dominion. Now I don't mean dominion over a couple of blocks in the neighborhood. I mean dominion over all. Did you know that you had this dominion and authority ever since God spoke of His plans for you in your life? If you don't believe me, then go to the book of Genesis, and it will tell you all about yourself (Gn 1:28). His first words to you were that you would be blessed. Then He said be fruitful and multiply, fill the earth, and subdue it and have dominion over all—over all the fish of the sea, the birds of the air, and everything that moves on the earth.

Now in order to speak, act, and think as a person under authority, you have to know who is in authority, trust in who is in authority, and believe in who is in authority. That's your power base in the spiritual realm. This is why the crowds that listened to Jesus on that day (which some of us like to say was His inaugural speech) were captivated, inspired, and even motivated as to what He said and how He said it. His tone was authoritative. He taught as one who had authority and not as the scribes (Mt 7:29). And He was also revealing for the first time what He expected of His ambassadors. Now you might say, "Wait a minute. I'm not an ambassador." Well, let me tell you that you are. If you accepted Jesus as the Lord and savior of your life and you can testify about how good He's been to you, then guess what? You are an ambassador under the King's authority to go out into all the world and make disciples of all nations and speak of your faithfulness. Then you are a spokesperson for the kingdom. When you become an ambassador, you have an inauguration service of your own and it's called baptism. And when this happens, you are installed into whatever the ceremony represents. Whether it's government or high office, you have been initiated into that organization. The Sermon on the Mount was your coming out.

Now shortly after Jesus concluded His declaration, He was immediately approached by a leper. And the leper said to Him, "Lord, if you are willing, you can make me clean." This was not a question. Judging from the way Jesus spoke with confidence and authority, the leper could sense that our Lord was in touch with a higher power. Not only did the leper sense that Jesus was able to heal him and make him clean but he also believed by the authoritative way He spoke.

I'm telling you today to rebuke the devil. Tell him that he's a liar and use the power of authority that is in you. In Deuteronomy 23:14, God said that He walks in the midst of your camp to deliver you and give your enemies over to you. So you see, He's always there to remove sickness, chemical dependency, and sin from your life just as well as long as you declare and decree the power of authority. Notice how these sickness and diseases fell into submission immediately when Jesus spoke because these things were under His authority. They had no choice but to obey.

There was a certain centurion in the Roman army who believed Jesus was willing and able. And being authority himself, he knew authority when he saw it. In the Gospel of Matthew 8:9, there's a point to be made of the encounter between these two authorities. In their conversation, he said to our Lord, "I tell this one to go and he goes, stay and he stays." And the centurion had the utmost confidence in Jesus's ability just by speaking with Him and believing Him. This enabled him to ask Jesus to heal him from a distance. No matter where, all Jesus had to do was say a word, and it was done. The same applies to you because of the authority you stand before. Demons and spirits have no choice but to obey when you say that name. The authority of the King was demonstrated over nature when He calmed the storm (Mt 8:23–27). He displayed His authority over demons (28–32), sin (Mt 9:1–8), and death (Mt 9:18–26). But don't try as people do to defeat the devices of the evil one without the authority of the Word. Sickness will never leave you. You will always be caught in a storm and be unable to navigate out of it. And death will sleep with you.

Jesus comes into our lives with hope for today. If you have died to sin and are spiritually incapable of finding your way back to Him, He's asking you today, "Do you believe I am willing? Do you believe I am able?" He has the authority to make that change in your life right now. That's why He came. That's why He's here—to transform and renew your mind. If you've accepted Jesus as your Lord and savior, then you don't have to go far into the world to battle serpents and demons. They're right at your doorstep and in your house, biting you, feasting on you and your family and friends. And the only way to be rid of them is by the authority vested in you. The Lord said, "Come to me and I will be your guide and I will lead you. For my yoke is easy and my burden is light." The yoke's on you.

In Jesus's time, yokes were collar-like, and they laid on the necks of two animals. The theory behind this was that the job was easier if it was performed by two oxen instead of one. And it was more advantageous if the oxen were of different ages—one older and one younger. The theory was this: the older, stronger, and more experienced ox could lead the inexperienced younger ox in sharing the burden of whatever it was. To anyone who asked God to reign over their lives, Jesus offered Himself to be a propitiation and be yoked and harnessed to those who called out to Him. In this day and age, you can find rest if you come and learn of Him and the authority He's vested in you.

Chapter II

The New Birth
Out of Control
Red Alert
Sinful Passions

The New Birth

What a wonderful day and age God has provided for us to live in. Everything around you is changing at a rapid pace. New products are continually coming out, but most interesting enough is the survival of products that have surpassed the test of time to be in sync with the day and age. Think about it for a moment. The technology is unbelievable. Cars can talk to you, identify you, and tell you the time and temperature of the day. If you want to know how to get somewhere, ask your car, and it will direct you and tell you the time of arrival. And don't forget your telephone. It can take your picture and record your favorite television shows, and you can talk to a variety of people at one time. And we could go on. The point is that new products are rolling off the assembly line at warp speed in order to stay competitive or merely just to function. The longevity of a product's ability to survive makes a statement about its inventor. From cars to telephones, new birth is actually a reinvention of the latter glory from the former.

The same goes for God's children. It's no wonder how we continue to remain strong, focused, and in tune with God's plans and purposes for us. The Holy Spirit is always teaching us, honing our skills, and making new improvements on us to keep us alert and prepared as new creatures for the battles of life the world brings to the soldier in the army of the Lord. Everywhere, you see examples of God's works in progress. Jesus sits at the head of the table, and we are at His right hand, making our enemies our footstools. And anytime there's an issue that needs addressing, all you have to do is go to the Lord in prayer. He always has time for you because His line of communication is always open.

The Bible says that we should examine ourselves (2 Cor 13:5). Do you find yourself spiritually sluggish, not getting motivated in the morning and having trouble throughout your day? Ask yourself, Am I really new and improved? Well, friend, I'm here to tell you that to truly be new and improved, there is a birthing process. Jesus said in the Gospel of John to Nicodemus, "Verily, verily, I say unto thee, except a man be born of water and of the Spirit, he cannot enter into the kingdom of heaven" (Jn 3:5). It's like pulling off the car lot in a new Cadillac Escalade. It requires a higher level of octane to run on the road, and we must continually feed on the Word of Christ to be new and improved in this life to function properly. And this is the same principle that applies when you ask God's Spirit to make new improvements in your life. You must be born again; He won't pour new wine into an old bottle. Have you really been born again? You may have a family member in prison, and you don't know what prayer to pray for their salvation. Has your marriage been rocked, and you don't know how to pray? You're about to lose your job, and bankruptcy and chemical dependency always knock at your door. Jesus said, "Let not your heart be troubled."

When you are born again, you adapt to a new set of standards—God's standards. His guidelines, His laws, and His rule book for our lives. When I was a boy, there used to be a gas station called Standard. It was famous because it represented the best service and the best gasoline. When you left that gas station, you felt satisfied because your tank was full. And the same applies with God's standards. If you got trouble in your way, pull into His Standard. The Holy Ghost will wait on you; and you'll get fixed, full, and filled with His Word. If you're tired of the way that old body is running, it could be time for a transformation. Do you need an oil change? Take advantage of your relationship with the potter and ask Him to place you back on the potter's wheel (Is 64:8). We are the clay.

I'm reminded of an old friend of mine. He was always the life of the party. One day, I was visiting the old neighborhood, and I saw him. He was standing on the corner, watching every car go by. And I said to him, "Brother, how are you? What's going on?"

He looked at me with a sad face and said, "Man, it's rough."

"Rough?" I said. "What happened?"

He told me that he'd lost his job after thirty years. The CEO stole money from the company, and there was nothing for him to fall back on—no stocks, no profit sharing, no nothing. All gone. He said so many people depended on him for financial assistance. His son was in jail; his mother needed medical attention. He'd just bought a new home and a new car in the garage, and then he said, "I'm about to lose it all. Even my girl walked out on me. What am I going to do?"

Ironically, this was the same friend that I had invited to church about a week ago, and he had told me that he didn't need that, that he was cool. I said, "What do you mean cool?"

He said, "I've been living this way for all my life. What am I missing? There's nothing I need. There's nothing I'm lacking. Man, I'm cool."

Sometimes it seems like everything is in control, like everything is going your way when all of a sudden, BAM! The bottom falls out. You've been hit so hard that it takes your breath away. You can't think right, and the little thought you have can't and won't change the situation that you are in. But if you go to the Lord in prayer and ask Him to deliver you from that stinking thinking, He will. But there must first be a conversion—a new birth, a new set of beliefs and virtues so the old man can exit and the new man can come in.

My good friend began to believe in the miraculous healing power of God after he'd heard my testimony. He attended church, confessed his sins on the altar, was baptized, was forgiven, and became a new man. Today, he has a new position and is doing better than ever before because now he knows that everything you do is to be done in the service of the Lord (Col 3:10, 2 Cor 5:17). But you first must be born again.

Whoever you are, wherever you are right now, pray and ask God to renew your spirit man in His name. All the doom and gloom that was before you will disappear, and you'll see things from a new perspective. Don't you think it's time you pulled into God's Standard station for a tune-up and an oil change?

Out of Control

Is your life unmanageable? How about the lives of loved ones around you? People who depend on you and are continually in need of your prayers? Do you have a drug-addicted child, and every time you see them, you have to hammer down everything because if you don't, it will be gone when they visit and you turn your back? There's something wrong with this picture. Do you agree? Has your prayer life been shaken so that you don't know which way to turn? Sounds to me like things might be out of control.

When we stray away from the guidelines (Jos 1:8) that God establishes for us to live by, our being drifts away into a state of spiritual unconsciousness, and we're lost in space and become residents of the twilight zone. Our thoughts are no longer our own. We lose sight of who we are and what our gifts are. And most important of all is, we've abandoned our service to God.

This is what happens when the sheep stray away from the shepherd and forget the laws that He established for us to live by. I would exhort anyone who's strayed from the flock to read the book of Deuteronomy, especially the twenty-eighth chapter, to get back on track. Brothers and sisters, remember that prayers go up and blessings come down. And you are always prone to attacks from all sides, being soldiers in the army of the Lord—be it related to relationships, jobs, or finances. When Satan sees an opportunity to unleash his imps and demons to prey on your flesh, he will.

That's why we have God's Words in the Bible to guide us, to get back to being self-controlled. There's a battle plan for every attack the devil unleashes. There's a strategy, a place of refuge, and plenty of ammo within your reach to arm you and fortify your armor and keep you battle ready for every attack. Sounds like you're armed and dangerous to me. And your weapons of warfare are many (Eph 6:11). Put on the whole armor of God.

RED ALERT! RED ALERT! How do you know when you are under attack? By studying God's Word, you are kept busy when the devil is looking for points of weakness. When I was new in the army of the Lord, attacks always came, and they still do. But God always makes a way. I learned that one of the weakest points in our armor is our dreams—the things that parallel our minds and our hearts, the areas that we let our shields down that hurt us the most. And I learned how to get the victory over night attacks that had me walking around dead and dreaming in the daytime. I learned to shout out and say, "Get thee back, Satan. I rebuke you in the name of Jesus." RED ALERT! RED ALERT! Are you receiving heavy artillery attack on all fronts and need assistance right now? Then it's time to pray the Lord's Prayer. Then and only then will the cavalry come. If you're at work and unable to focus, these are the mechanics of the prince of the power of the air. He brings thoughts into our minds while we are weak from night attacks. And after he's done his damage and your face is broke and you've lost all your hope, he stands in the shadows and laughs and plots your destruction, delivering the final blow.

All the while, God is testing you. He's already told the devil that no matter what devious plan he has in mind for you, they are going to fail. Remember when you were a kid and you would watch Popeye and Olive Oyl and that guy Brutus was always around. (Ironically, in biblical times, the name Brutus was associated with the dark side of Satan.)

Brutus would come in and beat up our hero, take or destroy everything he had, including the girl, and ride off. Then all of a sudden, Popeye remembered his spinach—that can of "comeback" (our spinach is the Word). And before you know it, he was in position to get back all that he'd lost to the enemy and regain even more. We must remember that before we go to take back what the enemy took from us, we must come back to the house of the Lord. Set your heart on what God has in store for you. Don't stand on the outside looking in. Come back to Christ. He's waiting. Haven't you been gone long enough? The longer you stay away, the blinder you'll become and the more confused you'll remain. Isn't it time to get control back over your life? God is an all-loving god. Say, "Here I am, Lord. Show me what you want me to do. I have strayed like a sheep [Is 53:6], and you have found me [Lk 15:4–7]. Make me an instrument of the Word, Lord Jesus. Walk with me right now. Open my eyes so that I may never walk in darkness again." Say, "The Lord is my light and my salvation. Whom shall I fear? The Lord is the strength of my life. Of whom shall I be afraid? Jesus, I need control over my life, not to be afraid when trials and temptations come my way, to say no to sin and yes to You. Restore in me the virtues that will produce a well-rounded Christian life through faith, self-control, and brotherly love [2 Pet 1:3–9]. Amen."

Red Alert

Red alert! Red alert! Intruder! Intruder! Prepare for attack! Prepare for attack! Shields up! Shields up! Brace yourself for impact! Brace yourself for impact! Satan has breached the perimeter! I say again: Satan has breached the perimeter! All hands on deck! All hands on deck! Battle stations! Battle stations!

Are you protected from the barrage coming in your life? Consider the never-ending war that's being waged against you by the forces of evil since the beginning of time. What's the prize? What's at stake? The answer to these questions is a sure one: it's your soul. Here's where being a doer of the Word and not just a hearer plays an important role in our lives.

By being a soldier in God's army, it's very important that you know your soldier's manual and speak God's Word daily—morning, noon, and night—because your enemy has a soldier's manual also, and he does not sleep. You are up against a formidable foe that will stop at nothing until you are dead and destroyed. His name is Satan, and he causes the world to hate you. And through deceit, his tentacles are far-reaching. He's caused the collapse of nations, homes, and families. And in most cases, he's taken hostages, defecting them and converting them to his way of thinking by using his very strong influence. He kind of reminds you of the most feared oceanic predator, the shark, who never sleeps and only lives to seek, eat, and devour all in its path.

But with God, there's victory at all times for all battles. There's one thing you can count on, and that is that when you go into battle to uphold His commandment, you secure a seat at the throne, an inheritance—the blessing of obedience (Dt 28:1–14). God gives to all those who diligently observe and do His commandments. Remember, the battle is always at hand. Attacks come by way of pain and suffering—family problems and family members taken away from home, becoming subjects of the street life, resulting in bondage, prison, loss of life, loss of business, loss of health, deterioration, and loss of judgment. Shall I go on? You know who you are if you're experiencing these kinds of pain and suffering in your lives. You are under attack, and your perimeter has been breached. Your shields are down.

That's when you know it's time to go to your Bible in prayer—the book of deliverance, the book of peace and salvation. There, your battle strategy will always be revealed. If need be, your armor will be repaired and made stronger from head to toe. You'll be reminded that God is the god of six wonders: love, peace, comfort, patience, glory, and hope. The stem of Jesse where a branch will grow out of his roots and feed you the understanding of the Holy Ghost and His manifestation sevenfold. God will fortify you and rain down blessing after blessing. He will bless your fruit, your basket, your store, your meat, and all the work that you do and everything that you touch. You will be above and not below, the head and not the tail. Remember, a strike can come at any time or any place. Remember, this is war. An attack can come by land or sea. But God is faithful; He will restore your damaged shields back up to 100 percent. He'll pick you up so He can fix you up. Just let go and let God. Call on Him, and watch Him show up and show out. Just come to the Lord in prayer, and He'll be right there. Rest in Him because God will get the increase, and watch how things will change for you on the battlefield. You'll get that raise at work, that home you wanted, that son or daughter delivered out of prison and brought back home. No more emotional mood swings. The world will know and recognize you once again. You'll be able to plant seeds again that will establish you a better harvest than you ever had before.

And most important of all, you'll get all your senses back. Christ clairvoyance is what we call it. You can see the enemy coming before he gets there, know what he looks like, and tell by the tone of his voice what his intentions are and send him back to where he came from. Know ye that the Lord is God, and His mercy is everlasting. He's the author of the blessings of life. There's nothing too big or too small for God to fix. Let prayer be the weapon you go into battle with against the prince of darkness and his crew. Then he won't be able to fill your cup with bitterness. It will continue to run over with joy.

Don't forget the parable of Jesus in the garden of Gethsemane (Mt 26:36). Despite all that might look bad for you, through prayer and faith, you can overcome all. Just place your mission, your life, and your purpose in God's hands and pray tears, and you'll get through your Gethsemane. In this war, battles are won by prayer. Lose your battle plan; it could be filled with holes. By praying, we establish our line of communication directly to the seat of Jesus.

So we must remember to put all our thoughts and wishes aside and surrender to the will of Christ. Only then will we stop fighting ourselves. We must feed on and have a constant diet of the Holy Ghost's power, wisdom, and strength. Pray continually, and your faith will never fail you. Your shields will always be up, and where others lose, you'll succeed. In life's darkest and loneliest moments, prayer will shine the light of hope.

Sinful Passions

One of the biggest challenges we face on this obstacle course of life as God's chosen ones are what we call sinful passions or motions of the flesh—one of man's weakest and Satan's strongest points. Everywhere you look, there is a sinful passion to challenge your faith.

Did you know that in the marketing and advertising schools, a large portion of sex must be studied before it can be marketed and used? If you look closely, you'll see all the hidden innuendos used to encourage what is called subtle sex. The jungle drums of passion carry strong, seductive beats.

And along with sinful passions comes a very dear price to pay (Rom 8:6–9). How can we as Christians live a righteous life, maintain a blessed marriage, and stay faith based if we become lost in lust? For you husbands, every thought must be taken captive to Jesus. Every thought of pleasure conceivable belongs to your wife. This is how God would have it to be. Remember, the flesh is weak, but the spirit is always willing (Mt 26:41). Through fervent prayer, your flesh will be transformed if you pray the prayer of faith. Brothers and sisters, we are facing perilous times. People have become lovers of pleasure rather than lovers of God. Let me say that again: lovers of pleasure rather than lovers of God. And sinful passions ranks number 1 among these pleasures. Satan dips his poison arrows and shoots to maim and wound his intended target. Vanity is a form of disobedience used against the children of God.

Man deceives with vain words to unsuspecting women, creeping into their households and hearts with lies and false promises. One thing after another, and before you know it, lust has given birth to a sinful passion. Sinful passion represents illusion, false hope, and misery. And if you hang around a little longer, it will rid you of your sanity, split your tongue, gloss it, and wax it with profanity. Be careful what you eat and what you drink and who you do it with because vanity is one of the false prophet's tools. Vanity is in your workplace and in your neighborhood, representing false idols. Vanity sends someone in your face, flaunting that jewelry they just bought at Saks First Avenue, not Saks Fifth, carrying that Cucci handbag and not that Gucci handbag. The Bible says in Job 31:5–8, "If I have walked with vanity, or if your foot has hastened to deceit, let it be weighed in an even balance that God may know my integrity."

God has a plan for you. He has already established a place for you in His kingdom. But you must maintain your contact with Him and keep the line of communication open at all times. Put your strength aside and place total reliance on Jesus. He's ready, and He's waiting. All you have to do is pray. Pray with the knowledge that through all things, faith is the answer. This is how battles are won against sinful passions. Prepare yourself for battle by letting your Father know what you want. Let your passion be Christ and not sin. You cannot be a servant to God and mammon. The treasures that God has set up for you are on the basis of faith. Consider yourself having a personal deposit and withdrawal with Jesus in heaven. Your riches are already there, deposited by your works, the seeds you've sown. But you have zero balance if you sow seeds of passion and seeds of action. Increase your riches so that when you pray to God for something, He will deliver through your faith. His personal signature will be on that withdrawal slip. Our Father wants us to be wealthy in Christ. But remember that wealth gotten by vanity shall be diminished. But he that gathered by labor shall increase (Prv 13:11). When you plant, God delivers. And when you water, then again, God delivers. He's the one doing the increasing. If you want God to go into action, pray. If you want Him to erase sinful passion, pray. And He'll come through and bring all good things to you in time. Just remember to wait on the Lord.

Chapter III

Drinking from the Chalice of Knowledge

The Messenger
The Family Business
Pharaoh of the Fleshhook
Crossing the Barriers into the Dimension of Truth
Chapter 7
Esau's Values

The Messenger

In every household in every family, there's a messenger or messengers, depending on your family's marital status. It doesn't necessarily have to be your mom or dad whom God gives the message to; it could be your brother or sister who gets chosen to deliver the Word.

In this fallen world, we know that there is no such thing as an issueless house. In reality, there are no Huxtables or Cleavers. Under a real roof, there are demons of varying kinds. You have the common garden type: demons of depression, demons of doubt, demons of social secularism, demons of love, demons of hate. There could be all kinds of sickness roaming around in your house. Your husband could be cheating. Your son might think he's a woman. Your daughter might believe she was born to be a man.

Mark 7:34 Ephphatha (which means "be opened")

Mary Magdalene had seven demons in her before her family called on Jesus to straighten her out. Somebody in that house was a messenger. And they didn't make any haste in getting the message to the source, Jesus. When He got the message, He came. As a matter of biblical fact, not only was it Mary who, as we said, had seven demons to be exorcised; there were other women and other households as well. For example, there was Joanna, the wife of Cuza, the manager of Herod's household. Remember King Herod? He sent the magi to find out where the infant King Jesus was so he could kill Him. So you know demons were in that house. Herod was the one who gave orders to have John the Baptist arrested and beheaded at the request of Salome, daughter of Herodias, who seduced him with a lascivious dance performance that pleased the king and his guests. If you want to know the conclusion to that madness, read Matthew 14:1–12.

Most of all, women who had to spiritually clean the house called the name of Jesus. And to note, these women supported Jesus and company out of their own means. (Read Luke 8:1–3 for women.)

Fellows, you know you're married to a good woman when she talks about cleaning up her house. That makes the demons tremble because they know what she's (Mk 5:9, Legion) talking about. She's about to call on Jesus. Now you take us guys. We have trouble getting the demons to go. In fact, we do more inviting than we do evicting.

We know how we are, don't we, guys? And our ladies do too after all.

We might have a bad secular day, looking for someone to pick on or starting a fight with the wife. So what do we do? We sit down with the demon Want Some Trouble, but that ain't enough. You see, demons travel in packs for assured victory. Now here, this woman is in her house, having been peaceful all day. Then here you come. So the demon Want Some Trouble gives you a nudge, but you're hesitant. So now here comes the tag team effect. Want Some Trouble whistles over and calls the demon Ricky to come over with some assistance. "Bring a glass. And also, you might want to bring the demon of courage, stupidity, and pain along with you."

Now this is how it plays out. I know a lot of you guys and gals have starred in this video before.

There you are sitting on the couch. Fried pork steak, greens and cornbread, macaroni and cheese are in the kitchen, cooking. Momma knows how to take care of her man and is a fool too.

Now while you're sitting there, you recall the demon Ricky. Well, his last name is Mr. Rose. His first name is Wild Irish. Notice we said *wild*. Remember when Want Some Trouble called Rick over to the couch and said bring a glass? If you noticed, he didn't mention ice. Now we know those of us who've gone up against the demon Ricky that he serves up a heck of a punch without ice. Really *wild*.

So now you got your baby in the kitchen preparing what might be your last meal, at least with teeth, while you're in the living room being attacked. Now that Want Some Trouble and Wild Rick have done their job, it's time for the closers—the combined team of Courage, Stupidity, and Pain. Now Courage has told you that Trouble said something bad about you and that he's hanging out with your old lady in the kitchen. And to top it off, Rick said she helped herself to your fragile jazz collection. So you go looking for trouble. And you're going to find it. Courage and Stupidity lift you up and point you in the direction of trouble.

You've found trouble, and you're about to meet Stupidity when you make that woman mad. And you don't want to meet Pain. So before she sobers you up, she says "Lord, I'm about to do something to him" or "Help me, Jesus." The message has gone up (prayer), and now we wait for the response (blessing, Jesus) to come down.

What we mean here is that someone in that house is about to become a messenger for the Lord. Something miraculous is about to take place. All calls have been sent out to Jesus, and He's about to answer.

That's just one of the many instances where God stepped in and placed the spirit of the messenger in you. You didn't know it at the time, but that moment of turmoil in that house became a blessing. Somebody got saved—I mean in the spiritual sense of the word—and became a messenger for the Lord to deliver the Word and plant the spirit of saving grace direct from the Father Himself into someone's life.

In Luke 9, Jesus gave His disciples the same power and authority He gave you to drive out all demons and to cure diseases, and He sent them out to preach the kingdom of God and to heal the sick.

Ask God today to send the message through you. Your word will be His word, as in 1 John 3:24. When you keep God's commandments, you abide in Him and He in you. You have overcome the world because He is in you (1 Jn 4:41). Put the message in the ear of someone you love. "Be God's Word" is your message.

At the Bedell Group Initiative, our mission is

- to be a community of praise,
- to be ambassadors for Christ,
- to preach the good news to the lost, and
- to aim for the heart and shoot to heal.

The Family Business

What gave me the clue that God was the consummate businessman? It was when our Lord, the most high priest, said He was being about His Father's work, His Father's business.

For a total of four days, He went missing. How He could have gotten separated in the midst of the festival of Passover, we don't know. Today His parents might have been harassed for child endangerment and neglect by the authorities. But this child didn't need the kind of supervision that most children do.

Yet out of love and concern as parents, Joseph and Mary and company doubled back a day's journey to find their missing boy wonder. For wonderful is what He was. At the age of twelve, He had become strong in spirit and filled with wisdom, and the grace of God was upon Him (Lk 2:40).

And after three days of asking, three days of searching, three days of worrying, they found their son in the local temple, explaining life to scholars. His parents had obviously forgotten in their haste and concern what the angel of God had told them about who their son would be (Lk 1:30–37). Yet out of parental concern, they sought to chastise him. When they found Him, His mother had said in alarm, "What have you done? Why did you do this? We have been looking for you."

Then He responded and said, "Why were you looking for me? Didn't you know that I must be about my Father's business?" We should be about our Father's business. For you are all sons of God through faith in Christ Jesus. Therefore, as heirs, according to the promise of Abraham, we should be about our Father's business (Gal 3:29).

We were all created workmen and workwomen (Eph 2:10) once unknowledgeable about what our business was, what our work was to be. We wandered around aimlessly, having no hope and without God in the world (2:12). But when the blood realigned us with the way (Jn 14:6), our spirits began to walk upright again through the good works God prepared for us beforehand. Did you know that when your spirit receives the good news, it jumps for joy? But your flesh can still be slumped over in revolt as if it wants to be dislocated rather than be restored or healed (Heb 12:12–13).

Your flesh would have you to be unproductive, ineffective, consumed in, of, and by itself. It is not for us to fear what the flesh will do but rather to fear what our God can do because He is an all-consuming fire. We wage war against something so small and insignificant when we should be controlling and winning on every front of this carnal battle. Remember, you have been loosed by the blood from the carnal mind to a spiritual mind. You have been loosed from sin (Rom 6:22)/8–11–06.

If you have been loosed, you have been freed. If you have been freed, you have died. If you have died, then you do not live to the principles of this world but the principles from above where your mind should be set (Col 2:20, 3:1), where your walk should be straight. So why are you spiritually bound? Why do you continue to look down instead of up? Because you've become a prodigal. Whether you are a prodigal son or a prodigal daughter, you've excluded yourself from the empire of the grace and goodness of God. Like so many others before us, we step out and away from the family business, our Father's business.

So what is our Father's business? What are we supposed to be about?

Change! From this day on, be glad in the Lord. Sing to Him as long as you live. Remember His marvelous works, His wondrous works. Change steps out in faith and knows no limits. It's time to put an end to being bound. It's time to come out of that spiritual closet you've been shut up in for so long. Unable to turn to the left and unable to turn to the right, trapped with debt closing in, trapped with loneliness closing in—all these circumstances surround you until you can't breathe. TRAPPED.

And you ain't got no room because you're stuck hiding in a closet.

I used to hear the young people say, "You better find you some business." Have you ever heard that said by young people before? They were issuing out wisdom and didn't even know it.

When the demons find out that you got yourself some business, they scatter and they flee. The victory celebration has been postponed. Because you found yourself some business, they got to pack up and go.

Jesus had some business when He was twelve years old. If you're thirty years old and you ain't got no business, it's because you're minding somebody else's business. Get yourself some business today. If you're forty years old and you haven't realized yet that the hands you got are for labor, everything around you is yours. Stop looking around for something to do, and do what you're made to. Lift up. Build up.

You don't have to worry about the high prices of living when you're about your Father's business.

You don't have to worry about gasoline for your car when you're about your Father's business. He'll make sure you have more than enough.

A certain woman said to Elisha, "I have nothing in the house but a jar of oil."

He said, "What do you have in your house?"

She said, "All I have is bills and a jar of oil." That was all he needed to know. You see, when you are about your Father's business, everything natural must bow down and make way for the supernatural.

God expanded her tent, and He will expand yours and lengthen your cords left and right. That means "make way"; blessings are coming, and you're going to need more room. He's going to provide you with more, enlarge your tent (Is 54:2).

You can't place a limit on what God will do when you're about His business.

Get yourself some business—the business of faith and abundance; the business of receiving; the business of being the head, not the tail; the business of lending, not borrowing. No enemy will be able to ever again stop your blessing. Don't you know your work is blessed (Dt 28:12)?

Walk like you got some business
Talk like you got some business
Dress like you got some business
Pray like you got some business
Cast out demons, that's your business
Heal the sick, that's your business
Feed the hungry, that's your business
Clothe the naked, that's your business
Preach the good news, that's your business

Stop getting trapped. See beyond your circumstances. You can't fall too far where God can't pick you up. Stop blessing blocking and prosper (Dt 30:4–7).

GSBN: Get yourself some business now! Shake yourself loose. Get those shackles off today. Choose life and inherit your Father's business. It's been handed down from your descendants to you. Possess it!

Pharaoh of the Fleshhook

"Um, um. I sho would like to get me some of that. There goes a hundred degrees in them pants. Hot! Gots to be mo' careful! See what red beans and rice will do for you? Go 'head and get you some. Ain't nobody gonna know." Sound familiar?

Don't act like you don't know anything about that. Don't be in denial. I can see your face now looking all contrite, saying something like "No, no, that ain't me. I'm a Christian. Yada, yada, yada." Well, I got news for you.

If it wasn't you then, Christian, then it is you now! Because we all came from somewhere to get somewhere. Amen. But pride of the world is pride of the eye, and pride of the eye is the lust of the flesh. Or simply put, if you lost, you're lost. So if you ain't coming yet, then you still gotta come. Are you one of those perpetrators who wear a cross and still run around lost? Here's an observation for you: I see more people wearing crosses outside the church than I do inside the church. There's more people who don't go to church than those who do wear crosses.

You might not wear your cross to church, but you sure do wear that hook in your nose—that fleshhook that tells you it's okay to wear a skirt three sizes too small. You come in waddling instead of walking, looking like a bunch of penguins. The pharaoh of the flesh says, "It's okay. I got hooks of all sizes. Big hooks, little hooks, large hooks, small hooks." Depending on the size of the lust, the pharaoh (Satan) provides the size of the hook.

An age-old device used to steer the flesh like a bridle moves a horse's body. The heat of the hot hooks makes your flesh a captive, a slave.

But when the blood was shed on Calvary, it loosened that hook right up out of your nose and onto the ground and freed you from slavery, from bondage of the lust of the flesh. Why did you go back searching for that hook? Because the flesh thinks for itself and uses fleshly wisdom. Leading your spirit in circles, the flesh says how, when, where. The flesh says go this way; the spirit says that way. The flesh says yes; the spirit says no. The spirit says stay; the flesh says go. You say you walk in the light. I wonder what bulb watt you use.

God knew that the world would lure you to put that hook back into your nose. That's why He said, "Arm yourself" (1 Pt 4:1) by watching out for false prophets and people who attract with words of emptiness.

Watch and pray, for the spirit is willing, but the flesh is weak (Mt 26:41). I guess my flesh would be weak too if I got jerked around like a rag doll and dragged in the mire like a sow.

Watch and pray because these jokers are everywhere. The apostle Paul gives a clear description of these "hookers" in the Second Epistle of Peter 2:18. He says, "They speak great swelling words of emptiness." (They tell you to "get out of them clothes, and let me give you some of this. You ain't my wife. Gimme some. Gimme. Gimme. Gimme.") They allure through the lusts of the flesh. (They wear clothes so tight their underwear shows, suggesting, "Get you some. Ain't nobody gonna know. Your husband won't know. Your wife won't know.") There are the ones who have actually escaped from those who are lewd and live in error. ("Honey, you better think about yo' self. Ain't nobody gonna know.")

While they promise you liberty (2:19), they themselves are slaves of corruption, for by whom a person is overcome, he is also bought into bondage. Watch when someone says to you—I hear this one so much today—"Let me hook you up."

Here's what I want to tell you: how can somebody promise you liberty when you have already been freed in the first place? Sounds to me like somebody's trying to hook you up.

Now here is where it gets good. Now if this is too much for you and you're still saying "That ain't me. That ain't me," then don't read no more tattoo ("The plane! The plane!"). Otherwise, let me hook you up.

In verse 20 of the Second Epistle of Peter, we see it says, "For if after they have escaped the pollutions of the world through the knowledge of the Lord and savior Jesus Christ, they are again, entangled [put that hook back in your nose] in them and overcome. The latter end is worse for them than the beginning. [When you go back into bondage after being freed, it's like you had a good home, but you chose the street, so you became a hooker.] For it would have been better for them not to have know the way of righteousness than having known it, to turn from the holy commandment delivered to them." But it happened to them according to the true proverb: a dog returns to his own vomit (Prov 26:11) and a sow having washed to her wallowing in the mire.

You see, when you wear that hook, it's heavy. You can't hold your head up. When you get loosed from it, you can see the sky. But to get crossed into wearing that hook again by someone named Criss, it's going to be worse because you went back to your own vomit, your own shame, your own anathema.

The Lord told you just like He told His messenger who visited King Jeroboam about Josiah, "Deliver the message. But don't return the same way you came." In other words, don't get caught up. Don't get hooked up. And what happened? He listened to man, and he got struck by a lion and died. Now this was a man of God. If you don't watch and pray, the same thing that happened to him will happen to you.

I'm telling you today: you've got to watch and pray. You've got to practice what's preached. In Deuteronomy 11:26, God said, "I set before you today a blessing and a curse [hook]." Practice one. That's when we got hooked. We got hooked on righteousness. We got hooked on truth. We got hooked on agape. Then when we got hooked, we got addicted. You see, when you get hooked, you've got to get addicted.

Stop loving the world and the things in it because if anyone loves the world, then the love of the Father is not in them. When you love lust of the flesh, lust of the eye, and pride of life, then you are hooked on phony (not phonics).

I tell you today. Get you some *business*.

Get hungry. Replace that hook of the world with the hook of the Word.

After you've been hungry, then you start liking it. Remember what we said in chapter 1. ("I sho got to get me some of that.") When you got some of the Word, you get hooked. You got to have it all the time. Now that you've become addicted, get your hook on by keeping your hook on. Don't forget you had to come from that place to get to this place. Now that I just hooked you up, you hook a loved one up. Now that I just hooked you up, now get up and go look in the mirror at that new hook you're wearing. Believe me; it's there. Thank you, Jesus!

You must put a stop to being led by a creature and serve the Creator (Rom 1:25).

You see, when you're hooked on the wrong things, you don't do right. But to you, it's all right. It's all right to lie. It's all right to steal. It's all right to rob. It's all right to cheat. Abaddon (Satan in Hebrew Rv 9:11) is so alive in today's secular world. Look at the news. People kill like it's all right. When you look at their faces or hear their words, they sound as if they got approval to be evil, like some unseen force—did you hear that? I'll say it again, *some unseen force*—led you with approval to do what you did.

I tell you, the spirits of evil are everywhere, calling you, pulling you by the hook. "Go over here and say something bad. Go over there and hurt somebody's feelings." You've been hooked. Now you're being dragged around like a dirty creature by a dirty creature. When a dog finds you, don't they take you around to other dogs? Creatures meet in alleys. Creatures eat in alleys.

Break loose. Seek the Savior. Don't you know now, every day is the day of salvation (2 Cor 6:2). That means you can be freed from being led around thinking that your past was so bad you've got to stay in it.

Don't you know it was God who brought you this far? And He said, "In an acceptable time, I have heard you. And in the day of salvation, I have helped you." That means today, you're supposed to stop being led around by the wise ones. That means *now* is your day of salvation.

Now is the day you walk by faith, not by sight.

By sight, you saw death. But by faith, you were redeemed. Keep on walking. You might feel like you're dying, but through the blood, you're still alive. You've just been chastised, but not killed (2 Cor 6:9).

Crossing the Barriers into the Dimension of Truth

Friends, I'd like to discuss with you today a word that shapes our character and morally defines us but also gives us a certain fear, a certain weakness, a certain timidity when it comes to facing it. It's called the truth.

We as beings in a secular world should consider ourselves athletes competing in the Olympics of life. And this particular competition will be the hurdle.

And in the Olympics of life, the obstacle for this particular event seems to be a barrier—a roadblock, one might say. But for the Olympic trainee, he or she knows that they can't compete at the next level if they don't make that hurdle over that barrier.

Now we observe that these barriers that stand before us are pretty high. And we realize that in order to get over, maybe we should recruit a trainer— someone of experience and knowledge who will train us diligently and look after our well-being. So after inquiries of fellow hurdlers, you're referred to coach. "Abaddon," they say. "He's the best. He's the king."

How interesting to see that these barriers we face have names, such as I, friends, family, job. And with each attempt to make it over these barriers, all ends result in futility.

Friends, the greatest feat accomplished by the king of the abyss was to get folks to believe that he never did and doesn't exist—that he had never been instrumental in the construction of barriers and the destruction of lives, morals, and dignity brought on by its erection.

Fueled by the inability to be honest with oneself, family, friends, job, and church, an invisible barrier goes up in one's subconscious (area of spiritual warfare) and blocks one's ability to express true sentiment and passion, rendering the receipt of this burdensome inability bound and anchored by the weights of treason, betrayal, and illusion.

Friends, the barriers we speak of here are known as deceit and denial, commonly known as lies. It's just like an actor rehearsing a line. The character the actor portrays is not one in and of themselves and is most times fictional.

Do you know that actors achieve honors by a rating of their peers? And of course, you know that the performance given by an actor or actress for that performance earns them high honors. But what is an actor? An actor is an illusionist. Acting is telling a tale in their best attempt at being convincing. Then the role becomes one's life, causing you to drift further and further away until the more you do and say, the more it becomes a barrier of sorts, distorting the truth standing between you and what's real. Let us examine, if you will, what makes it difficult to cross those barriers back into the dimension of the truth.

And the truth will set you free (Jn 8:32).

Let's assume that for every event that defines our existence, there are circumstances that can offset the balance of intent and reason. As we say, we go through things. In above terms, these are dimensions, with an entrance and an exit, that allows us to pass through to the next dimension or become prisoners in exile, stranded in dimenscia. We are stuck and unable to shake loose, yielding way to frustration. The end result is that one languishes and becomes a prisoner in one's own mind, unable to climb over the barrier placed before work with them (Eph 2:3). You can't go over any wall if you don't look up athletic trainers. Good trainers always tell their athletes during the frustration of training to always see themselves as having already overcome the obstacle. Sounds like faith to me.

Barriers have stood between man and truth since time began. This is no new occurrence in what we experience, especially the barriers of the four natures.

You see, there were no dimensions until after the fall. For so long as there was peace and harmony in living between Adam and Eve with God, then harmony and truth were guaranteed.

After the fall, all were shattered. After the fall came deception. After deception came death. And after death came the dimensions and the four natures.

Here we have sin nature, human nature, old nature, and new nature. Actually, these four are two in combination.

If you can imagine a meteor breaking through the earth's stratosphere at an unmentionable speed, the impact would offset the natural balance of the planet. This theory was introduced with the extinction of the dinosaur species.

So the principle here is that the old and the new natures are channels or dimensions by which our lives our controlled either by sin or by God.

Sin nature is old nature—the old self. The old man human nature is new nature—the new self, the new man. So we have old flesh = sin. New in spirit = saved (Col 3:5–11). But these sins are natural barriers that block safe passage into the dimensions of the truth, where God resides and you have access.

During the ninth hour when Jesus bled on the cross and bore our sins in His own body on the tree, the curtain was Jesus. Jesus is the truth (the dimension). The way, the life, and the curtain was torn in two; and the door was opened. The curtain is Jesus Christ. That is His body. He is the holy place. And the holy place is the curtain. And in order to enter the most holy place (the kingdom of heaven), you must pass through the holy place, the curtain of the temple—the body of Christ.

The first tabernacle was the Mosaic system with its imperfect priesthood. And the Holy Spirit was showing that by this way, the Mosaic way, it was not indicated how to enter the most holy place.

So therefore, when the blood was shed on Calvary, the curtain (Jesus's body) was torn in two, symbolizing Christ's opening the way directly to God (Lk 23:45) in the ninth hour. (*The Ninth Hour* is an upcoming writing we're sure at the BGI [Bedell Group Initiative] you won't want to miss.)

The dimension of the second tabernacle Mosaic system came to order when Jehovah, having sacrificed Himself on the cross, our most high priest, entered the most holy place (Heb 9:11–13) and made sinners perfect in holiness (9:14) so that you, too, may enter through that curtain, which is His sacrificed body, His resurrected body is the new covenant—the new and living way (Heb 10:19–21).

That's why He explains to us in John 14:56 that He is the way, the truth, and the light and that no one comes to the Father but through Him, the holy place, and the most holy place.

If you still don't get it, check your medication. Jesus was telling us of things to come even before his crucifixion. He knew it had to happen in order for the dimension of truth to be revealed. Hallelujah! He knew the effect of the fall and the blinding effect it had on people. No one could find their way anymore. The barriers were put in place to keep you from the truth.

When you look for the way, the way finds you to assist and guide you in your conquest to be a barrier breaker.

Before embarking on victory, King David sought counsel before the battle. If you missed the key to that last sentence, it's because you are still a captive to the dimension of bondage.

Well, it's time to break free! The wrath of God is about to be unleashed on your behalf. Jesus, the holy place, the curtain, is about to plead your case in the most holy place, where *no* is never said. *Yes* is always the response for anyone seeking a breakthrough. How do you get through any barrier? You break through! The proclamation has been given in the most holy place by He who sits above all. The mandate has been issued by He in the most holy place who sees all.

And when Lord Jehovah gives the order in your behalf, all hell is assaulted! When the trumpets blow announcing His arrival in your behalf, the earth trembles. Demons flee.

That's when your orders come down from heaven by the Holy Spirit to stand and see the glory of the Lord. Stand and see the deliverance about to take place in your life today.

From today on, your cry has been heard. But you must heed. Hear. Heed. Sounds like they go together. The spirit of truth is with you. And the mandate of your steps are in His hands. He's led many a breakthrough, and He'll lead many more.

Now is your time. Let the one whom the world cannot accept (Jn 14:17) size you up and suit you up for victory and for the godly life, the holy life, the good life you so richly deserve.

Know this though: just as the good life is about reaching out, it is also about reaching in, tapping in to all that is yours because everything is yours. Everything is attainable in the dimension of dominion.

It has been explained that barriers exist to prevent us from getting to all that rightfully belongs to us. Blinded by what was behind you, you can't see what's before you.

That's why victors walk by faith, not by sight. Victors win by faith, not by sight.

Here's where the spirit of truth sizes you up for your breakthrough. But in spiritual warfare, victories aren't achieved and wars aren't won without an increase in something. You know, like increase in numbers, increase in weapons, etc. Well, today you're going to be sized up for an increase in faith by decree from the most holy place. And the first mechanism to be used, the first blow delivered to that wall to break through that barrier, will be the sword of the spirit—the true weapon of faith.

Now if you strike that wall and nothing happens, you're obviously not going to get through. The weapon of faith must be increased. How do you increase that level of faith today?

Romans 10:17 explains that "faith comes from hearing and hearing by the word of Christ."

This comes by the reading of your Bible.

Now faith can be a very lethal weapon when used the right way. It's very dangerous when used, but relatively harmless when not.

What we want to do now is increase that faith, that strength that resonates from it. The key to strength and increase is by what? Exercise. A bodybuilder exercises regularly to increase his strength. Regular exercising in faith can bring about similar growth in spirituality. Remember, exercise has to be done every day to build up those spiritual muscles. Trim down that "fat" in the head. Train that tongue, and the whole body falls in line.

Are you ready to take your stand and behold the glory of the Lord?

You've been sized up by exercise. Now let's suit you up with the armor of God and the shield of faith.

The apostle Paul compared the barrier-breaking armor and weapons to the outfitting of God's soldiers: it's time to get into your construction cloths. Some walls are about to fall around here! We are going to set about the construction of destruction. Let's get our spiritual armor on.

The father of lies (Jn 8:44) knows what you're up to. Here's the catch. He knows he can't win, and he's going to tell you that you can't break through that barrier. He also knows you can win. But from his last encounter with you, you danced to his music. And being the suicide bomber that he is, he's going to hurl at your grenades of doubt and do drive-bys of despair. 9-11-06

This time, we're ready. The first thing you've got to do is protect your mind. How? By wearing your spiritual helmet. Then you've got to cover your heart with the breastplate of righteousness. That's where he's going next. You also have to hold your pants up when you're fighting. So let's get that belt of God's truth on to encircle us, that sword of the spirit, and last but not least, the all-protective shield of faith. Say to yourself out loud right now, "Devil, you're in trouble. I strappin' up in the faith. I know that you know that I know the victory has already been secured. You'd better leave peacefully. Now let the doorknob hit you where the good Lord split ya."

Let me tell you a secret. The barrier is in your house right before you.

Right now, I want you to gather all in one place what the world has used to keep you bound and captive—a secular prison in your own mind.

Get everything you shake your head at. Get the bills—even the past dues. You know the ones I'm talking about—the ones hidden in the mattress, the dresser drawers, the refrigerator, anywhere. Get the picture of that boyfriend who's cheating on you, that last paycheck, more past due notices. Now look around you: milk crate furniture, black-and-white TV with a hanger for an antenna, which shows more black than white, couch on three legs and four books. In your bathroom, when you flush the toilet, the shower comes on. In your bedroom, there's no queen-size, no king-size, just one size—mattress size. There's only a mattress. Trouble always comes in flocks, and sorrow has a numerous family. Now troubles are leaving with the flock. You don't belong to the family of sorrow anymore. Now say this out loud: "Up from me, legions of sin, armies of fiends, bodily pains, spiritual sorrows. You will trouble me no more. I steppin' out from fear and steppin' out in faith. And I will never be afraid again. Can you step?"

Continue this aloud: "It makes no matter what the enemy is or the number. Legions of doubt, up from me. Powers and principalities, up from me. Maliciousness, up from me. Spiritual wickedness, up from me. Stronger is He that is in us than they who are against us. Nothing can separate me from the love of God. I am a conqueror in Jesus's name."

Say it, "In Jesus's name, I pray. Today I'm breaking through the barriers of all circumstances and rising above the weakness of the flesh. Lead me, Father, into the dimension of truth and salvation in Your blessed name.

"The barrier of sin had defiled my body and made me foul and filthy, exceedingly stained and loathsome. Wash me, Father, as I pass through these broken barriers, leaving all the dirt and filth behind. Purge me. Lord Jesus, anoint me with hyssop so I may be clean. Let it not be in type that I am clean but by real spiritual purification that will take away the pollution of my nature.

"Let the sanctifying as well as the pardoning process He perfected in me. Save me, Lord Jesus, forever from the evils that sin had created and nourished in me.

"Heavenly Father, You have provided all that I need to live on this secular battlefield. You have secured victory for me through Jesus Christ's blood and canceled sin's power over me by giving me the armor of God to wear and protect me as I cross over into the dimension of truth. Looking back no more, from this day on, I will forever walk by faith, believing in my God moment by moment and remembering that my faith is my shield."

If you said this prayer, you have defeated the enemy, the father of lies. You have been cleansed in Jesus's name and have never again anything to fear but God Himself.

If you said this prayer, not only has Jesus secured ultimate victory over Satan but He also provided you with what's required for success in your daily struggles.

I don't know who you are. But I felt compelled to preach this to you today. Faith does not increase by accident. Growth takes time and dedication. The stronger your faith becomes, the easier it will be to maintain your position on the battlefield of your life. Ask the Lord always to help you exercise your faith today.

I don't know who you are, but welcome to the family. In Jesus's name, amen.

Chapter 7

I was at the bank the other day, standing behind two ladies who were having a chat. And I could overhear one telling the other that her life was one big mess. She was in so much debt that she didn't know what to do. It was so rough these days; she said that she didn't even want to open up the mailbox sometimes. Then it got so bad she said that she didn't want to even answer the phone. Overtime had been cut from her job. And she felt that she was drowning in a sea of debt with no remedy in sight.

So as we listened even further, her friend, the other girl, suggested that she file for a chapter 7 bankruptcy and all her debt would be erased. All she would have to do is pay a one-time attorney's fee. Then she could stop hiding under the bed, plug the phone in, open up the mailbox, and live. "Open your curtains and let the sun shine in." She wouldn't have to look back. She would have a clean start—a new beginning. And I got to thinking. I said to myself that with a new beginning comes a new way of walking, a new way of talking. You can see truth in your life. You don't have to lie to yourself, make up, or fabricate things. And most important of all, your life takes up new meaning. You look forward to tomorrow. You step into tomorrow with both feet on the ground. When she heard what her friend was saying, she had a charged look on her face from receiving the good news of how to remedy all her problems. I'd seen that same changed-up look on people who'd given their lives over to Jesus. After all, isn't He kind of similar to a chapter 7 firm? Cast your cares upon him (1 Pt 5:7) and all are forgiven. Just like chapter 7, He offers amenities. Jesus loves us all unconditionally for nothing. All we have to do is know Him, know that He is the way out of any circumstance, and He is the truth above all matters. And through Him, we learn how we should live—by being the head and not the tail. After all, He tells Philip in John 14:6 that He is the way, the truth, and the life. Here are seven steps to lead the way and show you the truth in life and wisdom.

And now I will show you the most excellent way (1 Cor 12:31).

One of the most, if not the most difficult displays of expression that we mask and hide so well, is love and its motivators. Remember the record "What the World Needs Now Is Love"? That song was sung by Dionne Warwick and was written by Burt Bacharach. It was recorded in the midseventies, I believe. And you know something today. The world still needs that love. This you know is true. If you went to a grocery store, for example, nine times out of ten, you might find in aisle 1 an impatient, fed-up, "mad at the world with no sex life or maybe a sex life but temporarily on hold because of an unexpected deterrent like an STD" single mom whose son or daughter just wanted a little love and attention. And this is what they're about to get. Now she takes the kid and whacks him/her like a potter placing clay on a figurine. Of course, we know with some children the crying escalates into a tantrum. It's on now. Now you got the mom and son slugging it out in aisle 1 of the neighborhood grocery store with the mom punching away. "You'd better"—*bam, bam!*—"shut"—*bam!*—"up"—*bam!*—"before I"—*bam!*—"kill you!" *Bam, bam!* "Embarrassing me in this here store!" *Bam! Bam!* All those head shots. Is this tough love?

When the police come and arrest the mom because a fellow shopper thought the mom was punching out a rag doll, the mom says, "I'm sorry. I love my baby. I didn't intend to cause a stir. I love my baby. Let me take him home and kill him." The poor child is sitting in the shopping cart, borderline unconscious. Is this what they call tough love?

I remember there was a time when a stern reprimand on the spot in the grocer, the shoe store, the department store, or wherever would go unnoticed. Why? Because it was the norm. I know I've been on the receiving end of a few. And you moms know what I'm talking about. As I heard one mother say, "I had to tighten that butt up in Payless today, honey. If I would have had a bat, I would have knocked 'em out. I looked around and settled for a boot."

Now you've got to go to school with a boot print on your face. You walk around and see people with looks of anger and hatred on their faces. I mean, wherever you go, there's so much hatred, so many smiles turned upside down. What the world needs now is "love, sweet love." What did Paul the apostle mean by the excellent way? The way of love. We know about the look of love. That's in your eye by Sir Isaac. Is he still around? Well, anyhow, let's examine the way of love. Bear in mind, this is about the way. Love is a fruit of the Spirit—one of the many fruits of the Spirit (Gal 5:22). If you live by the Spirit, you will not gratify the desires of the sinful nature (5:16). Please read Galatians 5:22–23. Character through strong Christian love is produced by the Holy Spirit and not by mere moral discipline. The indwelling Holy Spirit produces Christian virtues (love) in the believer's life. And whom we must seek is the spirit of truth—the spirit of love (Jn 14:17).

One of the first developmental characters that you have to learn how to adopt and express is love. Let love into your heart today. Let love go to work with you today. There's no need to fear any form of social secularism. The way is love. If whatever you do is not motivated by love, it accomplishes nothing. What people don't have is what you need. What people don't want, you'll have. Look at what's missing in people's lives without love—the patience of love, the kindness of love. It does not envy, and it does not boast. Love is not proud. It is not rude. It is not easily angered, and it keeps no record of wrongs. Love does not delight in wrongs but rather rejoices with the truth. It always protects, always trusts, always hopes, and always perseveres. Love never fails (1 Cor 13:4–7).

Of all and after all, there are three things that last now and forever: faith, hope, and love. The greatest of these is love. Because our Father Yeshua El Shaddai is in us, and He is love. And love lasts longer than all. The Lord tells Isaiah in chapter 30, verse 21, "This is the way, walk in it." In Proverbs 4:11, King David and Solomon say that "in the way of wisdom or just common sense, God will guide you and make your paths straight and add many years to your life." This is the way. Walk in it. Get started today. Break away from the fear and the seeking of social acceptance. You can do it.

Tap into your heart where the most omnipotent one dwells. In Revelation 3:20, the Lord said, "Hey! Here I am. Call me and I will come. Ask me and I will hear. I stand at the door of the kingdom of your heart. Open the door and let me in."

Tell Satan today his time is up and rejoice in his face. You're under new management. Say it every day, "I'm under new management." When Satan tries to creep back in, say it, "No, no, no, new management." The next time you go to a house of worship, look at someone next to you and tell them, "I'm under management." Start today, send Satan on his way, then claim it and receive it! Just like chapter 7, God is willing and able to remove all that hinders you and start you on your way in the way of love.

Esau's Values

Friends, I'd like to open this chapter with something funny I read the other day.

Some children were lined up in the cafeteria of a Christian school for lunch. At the head of one table was a large pile of apples. One of the teachers had made a note that read "Take only one. God is watching" and had placed it on the table. At the head of another table was a large pile of chocolate chip cookies. Next to it, a little boy wrote a note saying, "Take all you want. God is watching the apples."

Do you know what one of the most challenging things to do today is? It's something some of us take for granted with ease and with no thought of what consequence may be birthed by our action. It is the process of making the right decision. For some of us, it's hard. For some, easy. For some, it's difficult. For some, it's confusing. Some of us make our minds up instantly; some of us never make our minds up. I'm reminded of the story of Mr. Yesdear and his decision-maker. We all know who Mr. Yesdear is, I'm sure. Mr. Yesdear was the poor man who could never get out of going shopping with his beloved wife.

If you ever happened upon the pair at the department store, they'd be engaged in the most enlightening conversation you'd ever want to hear. She'd show him something, and he'd say, "Yes, dear." She'd ask him something, and he'd say, "Yes, dear." And on that sacred day that God joined man and wife together in holy matrimony, there are some who say his name went from Mr. Canobeer to Mr. Yesdear. I know in the winter months my wife likes varieties of gloves, scarves, and hat sets. Husbands, this is the key to being happy. Fall in love all over again with your wife at the department store. Remember she said yes to you. That was forever. Let your "Yes, dear" be just as sincere and truthful no matter how sarcastic it may sound. I'll never forget how one man I heard of went to the department store with his wife, and they went to the dress section because she wanted to pick out a new dress for a dinner engagement they were invited to. After trying on a number of dresses, she became frustrated in her decision-making and decided to rely on the judgment of her husband. So she asked him, "Honey, does this dress make me look too fat?" He said, "Yes, dear." And he was punished for that by having to spend an extra hour in the department store and miss his favorite television program.

But the subject of this chapter is not Mr. Yesdear. It's Jacob's older brother, Esau. Remember him?

Esau was the oldest son of Isaac and, according to law and custom, was in line to inherit a double portion of Isaac's possessions, including the covenant promise of God. This was his birthright—his right by birth.

But one day, after a hunting trip, Esau came home hungry. Jacob was boiling a stew of lentils, and Esau asked for some. Seeing his chance and knowing his brother as well as he did, Jacob demanded Esau's birthright in return. In the Bible, we learned that Esau despised his birthright and swore it to Jacob at the measly price of pottage.

What was he thinking? Esau weighed the promise of Jehovah's continual presence and blessing against a bowl of soup. Well, guess what? Esau placed value more on the soup than on God's blessing.

What could he possibly have been thinking? One thing is for sure: we have here an indication of his values and his character. Remember, character shapes values. Values shape character. The question is, Was Esau out of character? You might say, "No doubt about it. Of course." But quite frankly, his demeanor was in line with the time. He was in character. Now I'm going to hit you with a fact that's really astonishing.

Every habit, characteristic, and trait originated in Africa with the beginning of man. Let's look, for example, at Esau's character and people's attitudes today.

Esau was a man who valued the present rather than the future. He placed value on a bowl of soup against the presence and future blessing of God. Do we get caught up in the moment and give no consideration of the future? Esau valued the present rather than the future by selling his birthright on the spot. He was only concerned with the now. Do we live that kind of lifestyle today? We as a society today majority wise have no interest in waiting when something of value is concerned—or as we say today, letting something mature or grow. Our value, like Esau's, was for the present. Ask yourself, In what direction am I going? And where are my daily choices leading me? Do I so value my present situation and experiences that I fail to discipline myself to wait when waiting is best? Do I have to have the pleasures of eating despite the fact that I may be overweight? On my list of priorities, is God at the top, enabling me to spend more time with Him? Or do other things push him out of my thoughts? Have I inherited Esau's values?

One of the main reasons people reject God's love is because they believe only in what they see. They don't want to lose their secular grounding. You always hear people say, "I wouldn't have any trouble with religion if God made himself visible. If He became matter or something I could touch and see, I might not have difficulty in believing." I know you saints have heard this many times. It's the perishing one's best lines. But here's the clincher.

If you break down Hebrews 11:3, you'll see that God states that things that are seen were not made of things that are visible. Quite in line with Esau's character, not out of his character or his values. This is not a complicated explanation to how all that you see was made by the one you can't see. That at the time wasn't acceptable to Esau's character, and it goes the same for some of the sophisticated people who walk among us today.

If you stop for a minute and think, when God said in First Corinthians 2:9, "Eye has not seen, nor ear heard, nor have entered into the heart of man. The things which God has prepared for those who love him." What that means is that God is on such a high frequency that what He says and does only displays itself to receptive eyes, not rejecting eyes and receptive ears, not rejecting ears. That's why we say Esau was not out of character but in character of someone not receptive to God's Word. But today, one is out of character when the message of the cross is foolishness. First Corinthians 1:18 says that those people are perishing today. Are we not perishing today because of Esau's values?

Esau's values have molded and shaped our lives in so many aspects that the comparisons are mind-boggling. This virus was in the air right after the creation of man and is still with us today. What directions are Esau's value leading you in today? Are they leading you further from God's values and closer to man's values? Do we weigh God's continual presence and blessings against what turns out to be the equivalent of a bowl of soup, a new car, or a lottery ticket? Where does it end?

You can look at Esau's sense of value and shake your head and say, "No, not me." But I'm here to tell you that unless you make a strong effort and convert it into a daily habit, you might find yourself faced with a similar choice, and you might slip up and make the wrong one. Remember, you know in advance the choice to make, so beware lest you also fall from your own steadfastness, being led away with the errors of the wicked and the terror of Esau's values.

It's comforting and assuring to understand our position in the government of God as His forgiven people. And we should never see ourselves as mere earthly matter. But it is important to realize that however exalted our position, as we live our daily lives, we must accept responsibility for all our choices and act as redeemed people lest we fall. (In other words, live humbly will all men.)

Now when you fall, what falls with you? Your self-esteem and your values. Actually, you end up valueless, not value-blessed. As we said before, sit down and examine yourself. Meditate on it. Does it seem like you value the present instead of the future? Do you have a sense of valuing the material rather than the invisible? Does the momentary elation and satisfaction of physical desires seem to be more important to you than God's approval? If so, matter, the body, is dominating your scale of values, not the spirit.

It brings a tear to God's eyes when we see ourselves less than beings made in His image. Did you know that everything lives under a system of laws?

I am under a law—a law of morality that causes me to behave in a certain way. There is a law people obey in the streets. There is a law a stone obeys—the law of gravity. We are born under the law of human nature, which, in all actuality, is sin nature.

Sin nature narrows our scope and keeps us prisoners of human nature. Being made in the image of Jehovah God gives you dominion over all things (1 Cor 3:21–22). That means all laws are subject to your authority. All laws—that means the laws of the universe—were put on notice when you were created to acknowledge the presence of one of God's own. Did I not say the *universe*? Now this might be a little too heavy for you, but it's God's fact.

And that fact is, human nature does not acknowledge divine nature. Why? Because someone (I won't say any names) doesn't want you to know who you really are. And if you don't know who you are, you don't have character. And if you don't have character, you don't have a sense of value. Therefore, when you attempt to bring an area of law into spiritual submission, there's no acknowledgment of your existence because of your sense of values.

The result is disruption in your world. Your relationship—for example, the law of love—is beyond your reach and control. Your attempts to love somebody through harnessing the strongest power God gives us in agape love is lost in human nature, causing divine nature to give you no pass, no entrance into its dimension because your value is no more than the moment, no more than the material, no more than the physical. You appear alien, contrary to the divine nature of God's laws—the divine value of God's purpose for you.

The laws of your relationship and your finances will not—I repeat, will not—acknowledge you the way God meant for you to be acknowledged until your nature rises above and becomes one with God's values if you want to live in harmony with those around you. Your sense of value has to change. See yourself *with* instead of *without*. Call on the Lord and tell Him what you want. Take control. Take flight. Rise above. Poverty-minded to prosperity-minded. Open your third eye (your spiritual eye) and see God's love. Let it lift you up, change your sense of worth, and restore your sense of value so that the laws of the universe may work for you and not against you.

Harness the energy of agape love in your relationship today. It's God-given.

Stop human nature from dictating your values right now. Ask Jehovah Jesus to come inside your heart and instill the divine value of the divine spirit to uplift you and elevate you to your full potential. Don't settle for a bowl of soup when you can have the whole kitchen.

If you say this prayer every night before you surrender to sleep and humbly approach to the throne of grace and petition after petition and ask the Lord to hear your cry, He'll hear you and He'll answer.

Father, increase my faith,
increase my strength,
increase my wisdom,
increase my knowledge.
Reshape my spirit, like
you reshape the clouds each
day.
Restore in me my sense of
value, my blessed heritage
in the family of saints.
In your blessed name,
Amen.

If you say this prayer, it's already done. Now go out and have a bowl of soup in God's kitchen.

Little children, stay away from idols (1 Jn 4:2).

The Devastation of Accusation

For the accuser of our brothers, who accuse them before our God day and night has been hurled down. They overcame him by the blood of the lamb and by the word of their testimony (Rev 12:10–11).

Friends, I'd like to talk about the devastation of accusation.

Just last week, I was talking to a lady who was telling me how things had changed on her job in regard to her coworkers and their attitudes toward her since she let it be known that God was the architect of her marriage and her life and that she wouldn't be going to bars or after-hour places anymore. So out of respect, don't even ask.

Instead of receiving kudos and a "You go, girl!" from her coworkers, what she got was what amounted to the Christian experience in the workplace. What an eye-opener that can be.

People tend to get cold toward you and your God. They carry on like they're uncomfortable when you're around. They say things like "Well, to each his own" or, one of my favorites, "You know, I'm into that church stuff too." Folks change like a dog you just gave a bone to. If you ever notice when you give that dog a bone the way their tails and everything's comfidori. Well, if you try to come near that same bone you gave that dog a moment ago and try to take it, you're gonna see some teeth.

Well, if you want to see some turned-up noses and teeth at work, leave Friday for the weekend lost and come back on Monday found. Leave blind and come back with sight. You will receive the one and only one-of-a-kind Christian experience in the workplace.

The Bible tells us about the expectation of accusation and the Christian experience. Satan is always trying to attack God through you. Remember in Job 1 when some angels presented themselves before God and Satan was there also and God said to Satan, "Where have you come from?"

Satan answered and said, "From roaming through the earth and going back and forth in it." That's why in 1 Peter 5:8, we're told to always have self-control and be alert because our enemy, the devil, prowls the earth like a roaring lion looking for someone to devour and accuse.

Resist him by standing firm in the faith because you know that your brothers and sisters through the world are undergoing the same kind of suffering (5:9).

And in verse 10, it tells you that the God of grace who called you to eternal glory, not momentary, temporary things but eternal glory after you have suffered a little while, will Himself restore you and make you stronger and firmer against falsehood, lies, and accusations.

There you have it. Standing in the faith is an age-old practice of victory against the accuser and company.

Always remember, you are the focus of attack no matter the time—or as the Romans used to say, no matter the watch. You are never safe from accusation, be it the boss at work or a family member. When you stand up for Jesus in this world, you stand up as a stranger in this land (Ps 119:19).

Did you not know? You are a stranger, for God's sake. How can you tell? Well, if you weren't, you'd be very much at home as worldlings are.

You're not a stranger to God by no means. But you are a stranger to the world as long as you are out of heaven, your home.

And on the way home, don't look to be respected. Look to be rejected.

Always remember that you are a child of God, and that means you are to count it all as joy in order to be perfect and complete (Jas 1:2),

Don't let anything anyone says or does move you from where you stand. As long as you have on your spiritual boots, you're locked in place. You're standing firm. Holy ground is where your feet are planted.

And no matter how strong the winds of accusation blow, you will be like a tree planted by the water that does not fear when that comes (Jer 17:8).

Refuse to be accused by people at work who just want to steal your inheritance (2 Jn 8) right out from under you with slander and accusation.

The rules for holy living tell you to always let the peace of Christ rule in your hearts. And forgive as the Lord forgave you. That way, the Word of God will dwell in you richly.

When you wear love, you represent your ambassadorship. So whatever you do, however you respond, do it all in the name of Jesus, giving thanks (Col 3:17).

If somebody gets the promotion you should have got, God has your reward because you work for Him, and He's got something better planned for you. That person might have beat you out of a desk with a view.

God will give you the whole department. Remember it is Him you are serving (Col 3:23–25).

Don't ever forget one fact. Satan was under God when he fell, and he still is. He is not over God. The same breath that moves you moves him. The same fear you have of God, Satan has too. For example, in Revelations 13:5, four things are listed that Satan is given by God.

And as he is under our Lord, he is under you also. He can do no more than God allows him to do. In Revelations 12:12, a voice from heaven says, "Woe to the earth and the sea, because the devil has gone down to you. He is filled with fury, because he knows that his time is short."

Friends, desperation and accusation come in all shapes, forms, and sizes, but none are bigger than God.

Let's take a stand today and accuse Satan of being a liar. He didn't have sense enough to live in a good home. Who should he be that you fear he's a liar?

You have been blessed in so many ways. When someone accuses you or slanders your name, in Matthew 5:11, it says, "Blessed are you when they revile [which means to verbally abuse and accuse] you." And in Matthew, it says, "When people persecute you and say all kinds of evil against you falsely for God's sake."

God wants us to rejoice and shout hallelujah. Be exceedingly glad for standing up for Jesus in the heavenly realm. Realize one thing: the prophets who were great men were persecuted before you (5:12). When you look around and see all that God has done for you, there can be no words to make you depreciate all that you have authority over.

When you say, "Get behind me, Satan!" You're letting him know that you are aware and self-controlled, and you know he is not mindful of God but only of men (Mk 8:33).

One day, Jesus chose seventy men and told them to go to every city and authoritatively preach the good news. And He divided them in twos

(Lk 10:1). And when they returned, they came back with joy and said, "Lord, even the demons are subject to us in Your name. And they are subject to you also."

"Don't ever let accusation deter or distract you," Jesus said. He gave you authority over all the power of the enemy, and nothing, by any means, can and will ever hurt you (Lk 10:18–19).

Did you hear that you have authority over all the demons and their master? The next time you get accused of something, accuse the accuser and shout hallelujah. You're bigger than any accusation.

I'm reminded of a story I heard. I'd like to share it with you.

There was an old woman who came out of her house to get her newspaper every day. And she'd stop, look up, raise her hands, and say, "Praise the Lord!"

She had a neighbor who would come out of his house at the same time for his newspaper and make an accusation and say there is no God.

And this went on every day for a while.

Then hard times hit almost to the level of a famine. So one day, the old woman was out of her house for her newspaper and said, "Praise the Lord! Lord, your humble servant has fallen on hard times. Can you send some food?"

The grumpy old neighbor overheard her and went to the grocer and bought her a couple of bags of food that morning. He set the two bags of groceries at her door and knocked and hid in the bushes.

When she came out and saw the two bags of groceries at her front door, she smiled, looked up, raised her hands, and said, "Praise the Lord. Thank you for the food."

The old man stood up and said, "See, I told you there is no God. I went and bought those groceries."

The old woman smiled, raised her head and hands up. "Praise the Lord! Thank you for the food," then she looked at the old man and said, "and making the devil pay for it."

Index

A

Abaddon (Satan in Hebrew), 40, 42
accusation, 63–66
    devastation of, 62
    expectation of, 63
armor, vii, 18, 21
    of God, 18, 48, 50
army, of the Lord, 13, 17–18, 20
attacks, 17–18, 20–21
authority, 6–9, 32, 66

B

barriers, 42–49
battles, 21–22, 24
Bedell Group Initiative, 32, 45
birth, new, 13, 15
blessings, 2, 5, 17, 21–22, 31, 36, 40,
    56–58
blood, 34, 38, 41, 45, 62

C

character, 53, 56–57, 59
Christ. See Jesus Christ
Christ Jesus. See Jesus Christ
curtain, 45–46

D

death, 8, 41, 44
demons, viii, 7–9, 18, 29–30, 32, 35–
    36, 66
devil, 4, 8, 18, 48, 63, 65
dominion, 7, 46, 59

E

enemies, vii, 4–5, 8, 13, 19–20, 22, 36,
    49–50, 63, 66
Esau (brother of Jacob), 56–58
    character of, 57–58
    values of, 27, 55, 58

F

faith, 7, 19, 22–24, 34–35, 41, 44, 47–
    50, 54, 63
    weapon of, 47
Father (God), 24, 31, 40, 45, 49, 61
fear, 19, 34, 42, 49–50, 53–54, 64–65
flesh, 18, 23, 34, 38, 49
    lusts of the, 5, 37–38, 40

G

Gethsemane, 22

God, vii–viii, 2, 4–5, 7–9, 14–19, 21–25,
        29, 31–36, 38–41, 44–45, 50,
        54–55, 57–58, 60, 62–66
    children of, 13, 23, 34, 64
    commandments of, 21, 32
    the Father, business of, 33–36
    lovers of, 23
    Words of, viii, 18, 20, 32, 58, 64
gospel, viii, 3, 6–8, 14
grace, 2, 34, 60, 63

H

Holy Ghost, viii, 14, 21–22
Holy Spirit, 13, 45–46, 53

J

Jacob (brother of Esau), 56
Jesus Christ, 3, 6–9, 13–14, 19, 23–24,
        29–32, 35, 45–46, 50–52, 63,
        65–66
    ability of, 8
    body of, 45
    parable of, 22
    Word of, 14, 47

L

laws, 14, 17, 56, 59–60
Lord. See God
love, 19, 21, 32–33, 52–54
lust, 5, 23–24, 37–38, 40

M

messenger, 29, 31, 39

N

nature
    human, 44, 59–60
    new, 44
    sin, 44, 59

P

pain, 21, 30–31
passions, sinful, 23–24
prayer, 14–15, 17, 21–23, 31, 50, 60–61
pride, 37, 40

S

Satan, 4–5, 17–18, 20, 38, 50, 54, 63, 65
Sermon on the Mount, 6–7
sin, 6–9, 16, 19, 24, 34, 44–45, 49

T

truth, 40, 42–45, 51–52

V

vanity, 23–24

Y

yokes, 9

Printed in the USA
CPSIA information can be obtained
at www.ICGtesting.com
LVHW090823110524
779839LV00002B/563

9 781796 022230